The Boone-Bryan History

By J. D. Bryan

A great grandnephew of Daniel Boone

PANTIANOS
CLASSICS

Published by Pantianos Classics

ISBN-13: 978-1-78987-491-4

First published in 1913

The Boone-Bryan History

By Dr. J. D. Bryan
A Great Grand Nephew of Daniel Boone

UNITED WE STAND DIVIDED WE FALL

Published by
The Kentucky State Historical Society
Frankfort, Kentucky

COYLE PRESS, FRANKFORT, KY.

Original Title Page, 1913

**The Boone Coat of Arms,
obtained from England**

Portrait of Daniel Boone

Contents

The Boone-Bryan History

The following articles were read before the Historical Society some years ago and laid aside until the present demand for their publication was made. Dr. Bryan was a very careful historian, and has made, as the reader will see, a very careful and exhaustive research for data concerning his own people, to which research he has devoted money, travel and wide correspondence in America. His letter appended in regard to Bryan's Station fills a long needed page in the history of the Bryans at the station during its investment by Girty with his Indian allies. It will be seen a number of the Bryan's were there at the time. - [Ed]

To the Kentucky Historical Society:

By your energetic and enthusiastic secretary, Mrs. Morton, I am requested to write something "new and interesting" about the

Boones, or Bryans or both. As to saying any-
thing new, it is hard to do when the "field
has been harrowed" so thoroughly and by
more competent persons than your humble
servant; but I believe I can give you a few
new items worthy of mention, and think I
can recall many old, and so present them as
to make them practically new. As to this being interesting will rest with you.

Boone.

When we speak of Boone, of course we
mean Col. Daniel Boone, the pioneer of Kentucky. The history of the Boone family, prior
to their migration to America, cannot be had
but by a personal visit and inspection of the
records of England of past generations,
which would be here a brief, unsatisfactory
"record history," It seems that the first defi-
nite knowledge of them here begins with
the fact that George Boone, born 1662, was
married and lived in a small town about
eight miles from Exeter, England. Exeter at

this time was an important seaport town in Devonshire, S. W. England, and in their day (the Boones') was the seat of the old Saxon kings. In 1717 George Boone emigrated to America with his family, consisting of his wife, Mary, and eleven children, two daughters and nine sons. The names of only five of the sons seem to have been preserved, viz., John, James, Solomon, George and Squire.

George Boone and family arrived at Philadelphia, October 10, 1717. (It is said he was appointed secretary to William Peon by King James at the request of Sir Wm. Perm, M. P.) While it is generally stated he came with his family, there are records showing conclusively that some members of the Boone family were residents of Pennsylvania as early as 1685, and that his son George, was in Pennsylvania prior to 1713. It is also stated by historians that he came from Bradwich, England. This is a mistake, George Boone, Jr. (his son) came from Bradwich, The mistake has been made like loo many others that get into history in not closely distinguishing between father and son when of the same name.

George Boone, Sr., (as we will have to call him now), lived in Calumpton, Devonshire, England, and came from there to Pennsylvania. In that day religious beliefs were emphasized with much force. The Boones were "dissenters" and belonged to the "Society of Friends" (called Quakers), both in England and America; this was sufficient reason for their choosing Pennsylvania for their future home.

To properly understand what follows, it is necessary to know something of the political divisions of Pennsylvania at the time the Boones came to America, and trace the divisions immediately following.

As the grants for the Colonies designated some parallel or point of beginning for the north and south boundaries at the ocean front, and thence in parallel lines west to the "Pacific ocean," so the various colonial councils seems to have adopted a similar course in dividing the colonies into counties. Thus, in 1662, the colony of Pennsylvania was divided into three countries, viz: Bucks, Philadelphia and Chester. At a council held in Philadelphia "ye 1-2-1685," the boundary of Bucks county is declared to be a line beginning at "ye mouth of Poetques-ink creek, on Delaware, and go up thence by ye sd creek by ye several courses thereof to a S. W. & N. E. line [said line is the present south line of Bucks county], continuing said line as far as ye sd county;" this then meant to the Susquehanna river. All north of said line and east of the Susquehanna river was to be Bucks county. The boundary of the county of Chester to begin at "ye mouth of Bough creek, on the Delaware river, being the upper end of Tenecum island and 'soe' up that creek, dividing the said island from ye land of Androse Boone & Co., &c., &c ," from thence it meanders more or less, all the meanderings being given in the most minute detail, to the "Schoolkill river, which said 'Schoolkill river' afterwards to be the bound," all south of this line (the Schuylkill river) and west of the Susquehanna to be Chester county. All between Bucks and

Chester counties was to be Philadelphia county. Thus you will see all east of the Schuylkill river was Philadelphia county, to the line of Bucks county. It seems the first settlers of the Colonies would settle near the sea coast and form townships; when enough townships were settled, or there was enough population, the settlement would be erected into a county; a line running north and south would cut off the settled portion to the east, which would retain the old name of the county, and all west of said (north and south) dividing line would be given a new name. Thus the present west line of Chester county was run in 1729 all east retaining the name of Chester county, and all the great unsettled region west of said line and south of the Schuylkill and west of the Susquehanna was erected into Lancaster county.

George Boone, Sr., and his family landed in Philadelphia October 10, 1717. Soon after Boone arrived he purchased a large tract of land on the Schuylkill river and moved on to it at once; he had his settlement erected into a township which he called Exeter township. This is a short distance southeast of the present site of Reading, Pa.

I have copies of old records of the "Society of Friends" in my possession, from which I copy: "5-27-1713, George Boone, Jr., & Deborah, daughter of Wm. Howell, married." (Abington, Mo. Mt. record.) Again "8-26-1713, George Boone produced certificate from 'Bradwitch,' in Devonshire, Great Britain, of his orderly and good conversation while he lived there, which was read and accepted." "Children of George & Deborah Boone:" "George b. 5-3-1714. Mary b. 2-12-1716. Hannah b. 7-20-1718. Dinah b. 10-18-1722. Deborah b. 12-18-1720," "10-26-1720 certificate granted to George Boone & family to settle in or towards Oaley & join themselves to Gwynedd Mo. Mtg." You will see this is the family record of George Boone, Jr. Now note what follows:

"Gwynedd Mtg. 10-31-1717 George Boone Sr., produced certificate of his good life and conversation from meeting at 'Calompton' ire Great Britain, was read and received."

"Squire Boone, son of George, of Philadelphia Co., yeoman, married to Sarah, daughter of Edward Morgan, of same county, at Gwynedd Meeting House 7-13-1720; witnesses, George, Edward and Elizabeth Morgan, George and James Boone, William, John arid Daniel Morgan and 31 others." Children of Squire and Sarah Boone, Exeter Mo. Mlg.; "Sarah b. 4-7-1724. Israel b. 3-9-1626. Samuel k 3-22-1728. Johnathan b. 10-6-1730, Elizabeth b. 12-5-1732. Darnel b. 8-22-1734. Mary b. 9-3-1736, George b. 11-2-1739. Edward b. 9-9-1740." There were three others — Nathan, Squire and Hannah. Why they were omitted from this record I have not been able to learn. They were the three youngest children, Squire Boone being only eight years old when his parents died, and the other two still younger. As the new style of reckoning time was not adopted until 1752 in the British empire, these dates are all old style, and to get the dates comprehensible to us they must be rendered into new Style. If I am correctly informed this is done by setting these dates forward eleven days. This would give Daniel Boone's birth from September 22, 1734 N. S. Hence the State Historical Society observes the 3rd of October for Dame! Boone's birthday N. T.

It seems to me this record ought to set aside any doubt or quibble and fix for all time the birthday of Daniel Boone; also his birthplace, as it is shown here by record that he was born in Exeter township, on the east side of Schuylkill river in what was then Philadelphia county, Pa, But later (1745) "Berks" county was cut out of Philadelphia and Lancaster counties by its present north, east and south boundaries. Thus while Daniel Boone was born in Philadelphia county, he finally lived in "Berks" county, though he did not move. The want of knowledge of the territory involved and dates of organizing these counties and the similarity between "Bucks" and "Berks" is no doubt what has led to so much confusion as to where he was born. To settle another point, I notice in all these old records the finale "e" is used in spelling his name, and where they have signed their names, for any purpose, they invariably spell it "Boone." I have an old deed in my possession where Daniel Boone deeded a tract of land to my grandfather, signed in Daniel's own handwriting where he uses the final "e."

Again I quote from the old records: "Commission issued to Walter M'Coole as ranger of Bucks county 10-4-1741; Do. to George Boone, Esq., as ranger of Philadelphia county, same date." This was evidently George Boone, Jr.; we see he had become an "esquire" also, which was a mark of honor under the old English law, which then prevailed. Written in the old family Bible, by James Boone (uncle of Daniel), after Daniel's death (1820), is this, "George Boone, Sr., died in Berks Co, Pa., Feby. 2-1740, aged 78 yrs. Wife Mary born same place as her husband, died [date not given] aged 74; both buried at Oaley, Berks county." This shows in a striking manner how these mistakes of location creep into our histories; at the time (1750) this was still Philadelphia county, as we have seen that Barks county was not organized until 1745. James Boone further says that Squire Boone and his family left Exeter (now Berks county) on the first day of May, 1750, and moved to North Carolina, Squire Boone settled on the Yadkin river at Alleman's Ford, also since called Boone's Ford. This was in the same community where Morgan Bryan then lived. Here Squire Boone lived until his death and was buried in Joppa cemetery near the present site of Mocksville, now Davie county.

From this on the history of the Boones and Bryans are so closely interwoven that the history of one cannot be correctly given without the other. For this reason it is now necessary to "trace" this branch of the Bryan family to the settlement in North Carolina.

Retrospect: Ireland is one of the most ancient civilized countries known to history or tradition. Rome carried on an extensive commerce with Ireland (then called Iern), so that the seaports of Ireland were better known than the ports of Britain, yet Rome never attempted the conquest of Ireland. Nine hundred years B.C., Ireland was governed by a parliament, and the ruler, Ollay Fola, founded schools of philosophy, astronomy, poetry and medicine. Ireland was ruled by her own princes or kings from this time down to the English conquest.

Three hundred years B.C., Hugony the Great dividing the island into four provinces, viz.; Munster, Connaught, Leinster and Munster, which continue as political division to this day. During the first century a portion of each of the four provinces were cut off to form a "National District" surrounding the capital, after which our District of Columbia is patterned. The four divisions were four separate kingdoms; then there was a king over all, called "Ard-Righ," meaning supreme monarch of Ireland. As in other countries, these incursions were repeated with ever-increasing force until 840, when they had subjugated a large portion of the island and held it for seven years, when their powers were broken by a combined effort of the native princes under Nial III; but by intrigue, when force of arms failed them, they clung to the island until 1002.

The Danes broke up the schools and colleges. From these learned men who were scattered all over Europe and exercised no little influence in the civilizing processes immediately following. Kennedy was King of Munster at this time; he came of the old Celtic race that still inhabited Scotland, Wales and Ireland. Although one of the most powerful and last to yield of the native princes, the Danes had finally established themselves in his kingdom also. At this time surnames had not come into general use, though they were beginning to be used on the continent. Persons of distinction were distinguished by an appendix to their name, descriptive of some personal characteristic or location, as "Richard of Lion-hearted," or "William of Normandy," To distinguish the son of a man of note, a prefix was used. In Ireland the Celtic (pronounced Keltic) language was still in use, but like other European people, each little kingdom developed differences in dialect; thus in the Southern provinces "O," when used as a prefix, mean "son of;" in the Northern parts and in Scotland (where the Celtic language was still used), "Mc" was used to designate the son. Thus "O'Nial" meant "the son of Nial;" "McMorrogh," the son of "Morrogh."

In 978 Kennedy, king of Munster, was succeeded by his son

Bryan.

This name has been spelled in ail imaginable ways that the vowels could be transposed, as "Bryen," "Brien," "Brion," "Bryon," etc., but the wrong spelling most often met with in public records and prints is "Brian," "Briant" and "Bryant." Many branches of the original family are disposed to consider themselves a different people because of a variation of the vowels in the name or because of a final "t;" but I have evidence at hand that convinces me they are ail one people, sprung from the same source, viz., Bryan, King of Munster and all Ireland.

Bryan was born about 927; consequently, was fifty-one years old when he became king of Munster. As general of his father's army in Kennedy's wars with the Danes, Bryan had already become one of the most noted princes of all Ireland. Now that he was king, his own people rallied to his own standard until he was able to prosecute the war against the Danes with such vigor as to drive them from his own kingdom, when his fame became so great that he was crowned at Tara (1002) "Ard-Rlgh," or supreme monarch of all Ireland. With his increased power he was soon enabled to drive the Danes from the entire island, or confine them to specific locations and compel them to pay tribute, from which he was called "Bryan Boru" or "Boroihme," interpreted "Bryan of the Tribure." This has led many to make the mistake of taking "Boru" or "Boroihme" as his surname; it is only the designating "suffix." Bryan proved himself an able man of broad intellect, and instituted reforms that made him the most noted monarch of Ireland. Under his reign schools and colleges were revived, roads were built. He also built a navy and organized an efficient army. Among other reforms, he issued a decree that every man should take the name of his father as a surname; thus surnames became permanent and families were established, the family of Bryan, he in his own sons also established the family of "O'Bryan" and under its various spellings his descendants have figured as leaders in Irish history down to our own time. Bryan had a son, Morrogh (Anglicized Morgan), who in turn became a great general. Both were finally killed in a battle with the Danes, though the Danes were routed and their force and influence in Ireland forever broken.

Soon after their deaths rival princes got into wars with one another until a state of disorder reigned until 1115, when Pope Adrian IV issued a "bull" conferring the sovereignty of Ireland on Henry II of England. This is England's title to Ireland.

During the wars of the conquest, which now began, the native princes were killed in battle, forced to fly the country, or were executed. Many went to Wales, Scotland and

France, some with their old enemies, the Danes, now their friends, to Denmark. Many were taken to England as prisoners, or hostages, where they were executed, or after a period were allowed to settle as citizens. Being exiles and without a country, these princes soon lost their royal prerogatives and became merged into the citizenship about them.

Religious persecutions for conscience sake were now in full sway all over Europe. Meanwhile the "New World," America, had been discovered, which, by its distance across the great ocean, promised an asylum of safety and peace to the over-persecuted peoples of the old world, where every man might hope to sit beneath his own "vine and fig tree and enjoy the fruits thereof" with none to molest or make afraid," and where they might rest from the "man-hunt" of the old world. Among the thousands who came, the colonial records of Virginia, Maryland and Pennsylvania show that the Bryans came to those colonies among the early settlers in great numbers. They came from all over Europe, but principally from England, Scotland, Wales and Ireland. At what time our ancestors left Ireland I have not been able to ascertain; but from what I have at hand, they must have left during some of Elizabeth's devastations and went with friendly Dandes to Denmark, where I find — — — Bryan (given name not now known, but believed to be William) was bean about 1630, and his name spelled "Bryan;" this being so far back, his spelling of the name was taken as correct. He continued to live in Denmark until he married (name of the girl he married is not known, but believed to be Sarah Bringer), and had a son born (about 1671) whom he called "Morgan," after which said Bryan moved or returned to Ireland. After he came to years of maturity, Morgan Bryan left his parents in Ireland and came to Pennsylvania. You will remember Pennsylvania at this time was divided into three counties. The records show that Morgan Bryan lived in Chester county, where, in 1719, he married Martha Strode. I have information .showing she was a direct descendant of Sir William Strode, one of the five members who condemned Charles I and signed his death warrant. Morgan Bryan continued to live in Chester county until four or five of his oldest children were born. About 1728 or 1730, Morgan Bryan and Alexander Ross and "other friends (Quakers) obtained a grant of 100,000 acres of land on the Potomac and Opequan rivers in the colony of Virginia. He moved to this land and settled near the present site of Winchester about 1730. Here the rest of his children were born. The children of Morgan Bryan and Martha Strode Bryan were: Joseph, Samuel, James, Morgan, John, Elinor, Mary, William, Thomas, Sarah and Rebecca,

Martha Strode Bryan died about 1747 and was buried at the home near the present site of Winchester, Va. After her death Morgan Bryan sold his interests in Virginia, and in the fall of 1748 moved his family to North Carolina and settled in the forks of the Yadkin river, which was then Anson county, but m 1753 Rowan county was set off from Anson; thus they were in Rowan county. Thus we see Morgan Bryan had been living on the Yadkin river about two years when Squire Boone came from Pennsylvania and settled upon the river and became a near neighbor to him. Here Daniel Boone and Rebecca Bryan became acquainted, and in 1755 were married. William Bryan (son of Morgan and brother of Rebecca) also married Mary Boone (sister of Daniel) the same year.

These marriages of the young people produced a bond of friendship between the two families that led that and the next generation to share each other's hardships as well as pleasures, and that has not been broken to this day.

Morgan Bryan, Sr,, died in 1763; aged ninety-two, and was buried in what was then Rowan county, N. C.

September 25, 1773, Daniel Boone, Squire Boone (brothers), James Morgan, Jr., and William Bryan (brothers), and James Sparks, all with large families of children, many of said children approaching maturity, started from North Carolina to settle on the Kentucky river.

"Kain-tuck-ee" is a Shawnee word and signified "at the head of the river"; it never meant "dark and bloody ground," as is generally stated. These men with their sons, old enough to be efficient with the rifle, formed quite a respectable force, as they could certainly muster some twenty rifles. They proceeded without interest of note until they reached the Powell's Valley, where they were joined by five other families and "forty well-armed men."

Their daily order of march was for the armed men to take the lead, then came the women and children on horseback, then the cattle and young stock, driven by the older boys and young men, who thus brought up the rear and acted as a rear guard. In this order they took their daily march, and proceeded without incident worthy of note until October 10th, when they were crossing Powell's river for the last time, as they approached "Cumberland Gap." While moving, the cavalcade would stretch out on the road for a mile or so. The armed men had forded the river and were halted and formed in line to protect the company, expecting attack, if at all, from the front. While the mam force were thus on guard, other men were helping the women and children to ford the river. The time consumed in fording the river had brought the rear guard up to within half of a mile or less of the river. While some of the women and children were still in the midst of the stream the entire company were startled by a sudden and heavy firing in the rear; some of the armed men hastily mounted and rushed back across the river, and as they got fairly on to the bank, met one of the young men, wounded, dashing up, who reported that they had been fired on from ambush. The men soon came upon the Indians, after a sharp fight drove them off to find that the other six young men were dead. All had received fatal wounds at the first fire, showing the Indians had lain in the thicket at the roadside, and as the company was too strong for them, they had allowed the cavalcade to pass by, but when the seven young men came up, it was too tempting for Indian enmity to resist. They evidently each picked his man, took deliberate aim, and hut one, sent their bullets but too true, killing outright the six and wounding the seventh.

Daniel Boone's oldest son, James, was among the slain. Fearing a general attack, the company at once went into camp and remained under arms the rest of that day and night. This caused them, after burying the dead, to retreat to the settlements on Cinch river, Va,, forty miles back on the road they had come.

Here they erected cabins for their protection and comfort and went into winter quarters to await the following spring to renew their journey. The next spring an Indian war broke out, known as Dunmore's War, Boone was commissioned captain in the Virginia militia and placed m command of three contiguous forts, part of a system of forts from the Potomac to the south line. The emigrants remained in their cabins on the Cinch river during this war, which was concluded by the battle of Point Pleasant, October, 1774, after which the militia being disbanded, Boone returned to the camp on the Cinch. An impetus was now given to the settlement of Kentucky because of the bounty lands given her soldiery by Virginia.

Among many others, Col. Richard Henderson organized a company with the purpose of purchasing the right of the Cherokee Indians (whatever that right might be) to all the land bounded by the Ohio, Kentucky and Cumberland rivers. (Kentucky river was originally called the Louisiana river.) Because of his influence with the Indians, Capt. Boone engaged and went with Col. Henderson to attend a treaty with the Cherokees at Fort Watauga, situated on a branch of the Holston river. March 1775, where the right of the Cherokees to the above stated lands was purchased by this company. Then it was important to take possession of the territory. Capt. Boone was engaged to do this. He raised a company of well-armed men (no doubt his own people formed a good part of it) and proceeded at once to "blaze" a road to the Kentucky river. They proceeded with such dispatch as to begin April 1st the erection of the "Stockade Fort," which in honor of Boone, was called "Boone's Borough," on the Kentucky river at the mouth of Otter creek. The fort was completed the 14th of the following June, As soon as the fort was completed Boone started to the Cinch settlement for his family, leaving a small guard in the fort. The old company, William, James and Morgan Bryan, Squire Boone and James Sparks and families — and now that the danger was trifling, other families joined the caravan — in September or October, just two years from their first start, crossed Powell's river and this time proceeded to the Kentucky river without incident.

While the Boones proceeded at once to Boone's Borough, the Bryans only stopped there while they could erect a fort for their protection. They proceeded further north on the Elkhorn, where they erected a stockade fort, which they called Bryan's Station, which was built that fall and winter. Col. Richard Calaway and Col. Benjamin Logan, old friends of the Bryans and Boones in North Carolina, came with their families early the next spring (1776) and each erected a station or fort, as they were called both ways. These settlements were four hundred miles beyond the frontiers of Virginia and North Carolina. The Revolution had begun by the battles of Lexington and Concord. A company of hunters were camped on the present site of Lexington, Ky.; hearing of the battle of Lexington, they called their place "Camp Lexington." Thus came the name, and in due time, the town of Lexington. — These pioneers are now called the near guard of the Revolution.

As to the defense of Bryan's Station: My great grandfather, James Bryan (son of Morgan Bryan and brother to William Bryan), married Rebecca Enox in North Carolina in 1756. Their children were; David, born October 29, 1757; Jonathan, born July 15, 1759; Henry, born January 15, 1761; Susannah, born April 11, 1763; Mary; born December 13, 1765; Rebecca, born March 1, 1767. Soon after the birth of the last of these children, James' wife, Rebecca, died and left him a widower in the prime of life, about the age of forty-four years. He never married again, but lived a widower until his death, about August 18, 1807.

You will remember that Morgan Bryan's daughter, Rebecca (sister to James, William and Morgan, Jr., and the rest), married Col. Danie! Boone. She seems to have been a favorite sister with James, and after the death of his wife, his sister, Rebecca Bryan Boone, took his children and raised them and "Uncle Dan'ls" was their home until they were grown and married. The girls were all married at "Uncle Dan'ls" house. This circumstance begot a more intimate friendship between these two families than the rest that extended to the next generation, so that when Daniel Boone came to Missouri, James Bryan and all, or nearly all, of the children of both families soon followed him to Missouri, and there they lived within a mile of each other until the death of James, Rebecca B. Boone and Daniel. The latter lived until my father was a young man grown, and when about eighteen years old, actually made his home in Boone's house for about eighteen months to have "Uncle Dan'l" doctor his old snake-bite, having been bitten by a rattlesnake when about twelve years old, which had never healed. My father lived until I was about fifty or more; I did not leave home for good until I was past twenty-six, so you can now see what my chances were for learning the old family traditions. As I remember my father in his prime, he stood six feet one, weighing 185 to 190 pounds, a Roman nose, of fine portly appearance, and I must say of more than the average intelligence. Where I have found it necessary to verify father's traditions by search of public records I have so uniformly found them correct that I take them as correct, unless there is record evidence to the contrary. In the move from North Carolina James Bryan went with Boone to Kentucky and took all his children.

They stopped at Boonesborough until Bryan's Station was ready for their occupancy, when they, with others, went there and after that Bryan's Station was their home through all the Indian troubles from the time of its building in the fall of 1775 until they came to Missouri. In the troubles with the Indians in 1777 and 1778, many of the families who had come out to Kentucky, went back for safety, and returned at a later date; hence William Bryan is said to have "brought his family to Kentucky in 1780" while we know he came first in 1775 with Boone and helped build Bryan's Station. So with Morgan Bryan, Jr. This is how there is such a discrepancy among the descendants as to the time that generation did come to Kentucky. James Bryan never went back, but remained in Kentucky through all the trouble, and all his children. Thus he, at the age of about fifty-five to sixty, and his sons (Jonathan, my grandfather one of them), just young men grown, became defenders of the old fort in 1782. These, our grand aunts, his daughters, as young women, helped carry the water that historic morning; also my grandmother, then a young woman. This we know like we know many other things pertaining thereto — by father having many,

many times recited these facts in our presence, he having gotten them from his father and grandfather and Daniel Boone and others of the older people who did know of and participated in them.

At the time Col. Campbell, of Virginia (Kentucky then Virginia Territory) and others gathered up the militia (we call them now State troops) for the Kings Mountain affair, James and Morgan, Jr. (Bryan) went with that force and were at the Battle of Kings Mountain October, I 780; on the return of this force, many like my great grandfather and his brother, being from North Carolina, many of the families who had previously gone back to North Carolina for safety— now that affairs in North Carolina were so disturbed — took advantage of this safe escort to return to Kentucky. As stated, this making the second "going to Kentucky" for many of the families of the relations, thus giving rise to such conflicting accounts of the time the various families went to Kentucky.

Again, on the first trip (1773), after the attack by the Indians, on their approach to Cumberland Gap, where James Boone, oldest son of Daniel Boone was killed, the entire company retreated back to the settlements on Cinch river, Virginia, where they stayed two years; then in 1775 started from Cinch river, Virginia, and went to Kentucky. Hence some claim their ancestry came from Virginia, while others claim it came from North Carolina — all the same company, the discrepancy arising for want of the proper knowledge of the circumstances and facts. At the time of the attack here mentioned the company was fording Powell's river. Elizabeth Sparks (one of the five families from North Carolina), then about nine years old, was riding a gentle horse and carrying a baby brother before her. She was in the midst of the river when the Indians fired on the rear guard. My great uncle, Henry Bryan, at a later day, married this Elizabeth Sparks in Kentucky, and they afterward came to Missouri, where they lived until their death. She lived to be nearly one hundred years old. I have seen and heard her talk often. She finally died at my oldest sister's house after I was grown. Among these old people we get our traditions. I have also often been at the grave where Daniel Boone and wife were first buried in Missouri. It was right near where we lived when I was a boy.

Though the "half has not been told," having already transgressed my limit, unavoidably, it seems to me, I must now leave you on this historic ground where the Bryans and Boones, their relations and descendants were the founders of a great State; where the women, descendants of these, have long since become famous for their faithfulness, patriotism, intelligence and beauty.

J. D. BRYAN.

Republished from the Register of the Kentucky State Historical Society 1905, Vol. 5, No. 9.

Notes from the "History of Ireland."

Page 141:

"Castle Connell," on the road from Dublin to Limerick, lies on the right of the road and close to the rapids of Doonass, one of the most beautiful parts of the river Shannon. It is greatly resorted to by the citizens of Limerick as summer quarters, and by the trades-people on Sundays and holidays, to drink the waters of the Chalybeate Spa and enjoy the beauties of the place. The ruins of the castle, once the seat of the O'Brien, kings of Munster, rising on a detached rock in the town, from a very picturesque object."

On page 149:

"Three miles from Thurles, on the banks of the Suir, is Holy Cross Abbey, one of the finest remains of the pointed style of architecture in Ireland, founded in the year 1182 by Donald O'Brien, King of Limerick.

"By the Owne river is Birchfield's Castle, the residence of Lord Cornelius O'Brien. The tourist will observe the improvements effected by Mr. O'Brien, M. P., not merely within the boundaries of the grounds attached to his castle, but throughout his estate. There are various drives and walks along the cliffs; the stables, coach houses and splendid banqueting rooms will abundantly testify. To attempt a minute description of the cliffs of Moher (on the Owne river) is impossible. Suffice it to say, that they extend from Hogshead Bay to Doolin Bay, a distance of five miles, rise perpendicularly from two to eight hundred feet above the ocean and display all that wonderful and striking variety of awfully impending cliff, deep ravine, resounding cavern and detached island rock arched and pinnacled in a thousand grotesque forms, which the cliffs here in common with all those composed of flint and clay rock exhibit, when exposed to the ceaseless fury of a heavy sea."

The castle is near this wonderfully beautiful scenery on the ocean.

Additional Facts about Boone

(See Register Kentucky State Historical Society No. 1, Vol. 1 by Mrs. Jennie C. Morton)

It is with Daniel Boone as Revolutionary soldier, path-finder, pioneer, legislator in Kentucky and, later on, as Commandant and Judge Advocate under the Spanish Government in Missouri, the interest lies in this sketch, and, having given his genealogy, we pass on, leaving for another time a more complete record of the Boones.

Daniel Boone was born in Berks county. Pa., and not in Maryland, as is stated in Marshall's History of Kentucky; and in 1734, and not in 1746 as Marshall writes. Says Dr. Bryan again: "The want of a knowledge of the territory involved, and dates of organizing these counties (Philadelphia, Lancaster, Berks and Bucks), is, no doubt, the reason which has led to so much confusion as to his birthplace. Thus, while Daniel Boone was born in Exeter township, east side of the

Schuylkill river, Philadelphia county, he lived in Berks county, which was taken from Philadelphia county, though he did not move from said county. Squire Boone and his family left Exeter (now Berks county) on the first day of May, 1750, and moved to North Carolina. He settled on the Yadkin river, at Alleman's Ford, also called Boone's Ford. This was in the same community where Morgan Bryan then lived. Had been there about two years when Squire Boone came from Pennsylvania and settled near him, on the forks of the Yadkin river. Here Daniel Boone met Rebecca Bryan, the daughter of Morgan Bryan, They were married in the year 1755, as was also her brother, William Bryan, married to Mary Boone the sister of Daniel Boone, the same year.

The career of Daniel Boone from this time is familiar to the school children of America, who have the stories as pioneers during the Revolution. It reads like a romance of some ideal of a pioneer and discoverer, and yet Is beyond this in facts. From boyhood he loved the forests. He delighted to chase the wild deer and the antelope, and to sit upon remote mountain heights, and in the sublime solitude of nature commune with her in her silent temples and leaf-covered shrines. Fie was not a student, nor was he ignorant of books. He used his bright, deep blue eyes and his ears to see and to hear what was most beautiful and sublime in Nature, and listen with attentive heart to music that enchants or noise that startles, or whisperings that interpreted themselves alone to him for pleasure or for warning. This much we learn from his remarkable autobiography, written by Filson at Daniel Boone's dictation.

Says Marshall, in his *History of Kentucky,* vol. 1, pages 17 and 18: "accustomed to be much alone, he acquired the habit of contemplation and of self-possession. His mind was not of the most ardent nature, nor does he ever seem to have sought knowledge through the medium of books. Naturally his sagacity was considerable, and as a woodsman he was soon expert, and ultimately super-eminent. Far from ferocity, his temper was mild, humane and charitable; his manners gentle, his address conciliating, his heart open to friendship and hospitality; yet his most remarkable quality was an enduring and unshakable fortitude."

As Daniel Boone was living when this description was written, and as he was known to the historian personally, we quote again from him the following: "Daniel Boone, yet living, is unknown to his full fame. From the country of his choice (and his discovery) and of his fondest predilection he has been banished by difficulties he knew not how to surmount, and is now a resident of the Missouri, a Spanish territory. Nor will the lapse of time, in which fancy often finds her storehouse of materials for biography, much less the rigid rules of modern history, permit the aid of imagination to magnify his name with brilliant epithets, or otherwise adorn a narrative of simple facts."

Presto! The historian was a prophet; Daniel Boone has transcended in fame every American but Washington. The pathos of his singular life of peril and adventure is beyond the flight of poet's fancy or novelist's conception to describe or illustrate. Oratory has been taxed for a hundred years to pay tribute to his sublime courage and fortitude; history has adorned her pages with accounts of his adventures as a Revolutionary soldier and his discoveries in the wilderness of Kentucky; his wars with the Indians; his capture and imprisonment; his gallantry and heroism; his Christian fortitude under the loss of his darling sons and brothers and the ingratitude and treachery of those he had defended and protected with his life. At last the loss of the home he had purchased with his life-blood, and the lands he had settled in the State, his bravery and sagacity had held for the unpatriotic but educated statesmen who followed his trail and advantaged themselves by his want of knowledge of the Kentucky laws and deceptive technicalities. But honors were lavished upon him. By Lord Dunmore, the last Colonial Governor of Virginia, he was commissioned colonel, and many important trusts were confided to him as a surveyor and guide. He was a member of the first Legislature ever convened in the Territory of Kentucky. His judgment was appealed to in matters of common law and honesty, and he was supreme in command of woodcraft and path finding in the wilderness.

In a review of the Courier-Journal of the late Prof. Ranck's "History of Boonesborough," we find the following in regard to the Transylvania Company: "The two men who stand out most conspicuously in this great movement are Richard Henderson, who organized the Transylvania Company, and Daniel Boone, who blazed the way for its planting upon Kentucky soil. Daniel Boone was sent forward to mark the route and to select the seat of Government on the south bank of the Kentucky river, which he did, making the location at the mouth of Otter creek, in the present county of Madison, about twelve miles north of Richmond. The site was first known as Boonesboro. Here a government was formed, with Henderson for Governor. In May, 1775, a Legislature assembled, and in the Journal before us, which reads thus:

"Journal of the Proceedings
of the

House of Delegates or Representatives of the Colony of Transylvania. Begun on Tuesday, 23d of May, in the year of our Lord Christ 1775, and in the 15th year of the reign of His Majesty, King of Great Britain.' We find first among the names of those present, Daniel Boone and his brother Squire Boone."

Says the reviewer quoted above: "History records few such incidents as the assembling of this body in the primeval forests, 500 miles away from any similar organization. Although the grant (to the Henderson Company) was annulled by the Governments of Virginia and South Carolina, and the life of Transylvania was limited to little more than a year, the influence of such an organization under the forms of law, and of the educated men who directed it, cannot be overlooked" in Revolutionary times. It was the key to the possession of the rich territory of Kentucky, and no history can record more thrilling experiences of danger and difficulty than those Daniel Boone and his little band of pioneers encountered in their brave determination to hold the fair land they had founded. It was then that the pioneers found in Daniel Boone 'a safe guide and wise counsellor in every emergency, for his judgment and penetration were proverbially correct.' Though not a Joshua in might or mind, yet, like one inspired, was his utter fearlessness, his disregard of personal danger and his noble self-sacrifice, as evidenced in his terrible journey after his escape from the Indians, to save Boonesborough. He was 160 miles from the doomed fort, but when he saw four hundred and fifty Indian warriors in their fiendish paint and feathers, armed and ready to march upon the fort, so wholly unprepared for attack or battle, he resolved upon escape to warn and to save, if possible, his doomed comrades and friends. With one meal of corn in pocket, he stole away from his brutal captors, and for five days, without rest by day or night, he pursued his pathless way through the forests to Kentucky. He found the fort as he had feared — wholly unprepared for the savages. He began immediate preparations for defense. With the tragic events of this noted siege at Boonesborough, in the fall of 1778, every reader of American history during the Revolution is now acquainted. The pioneers' successful resistance, on the verge of starvation, of the assaults of the infuriated Indians under Duquesne for nine days reads like a miracle. The result was a blood-bought victory that eventually insured the safety of the fort, and not only that but it sealed the fate of the British army in Kentucky. It is said, 'Had Boonesborough surrendered, the Indians and British would have rushed through the forests of Kentucky unobstructed, to the rear of the army of the Colonist in Virginia and the East, and it is easy to conjecture the result at that time. The poor, discouraged, half-beaten and half-starved Army of the Revolution could not have contended with a victorious foe, flushed with success and booty.' So we may regard Boonesboro, with Daniel Boone for its inspiring captain in defense, as the salvation of the Revolutionary army in that year, and a factor in its conquest over the army of Great Britain shortly after He was, after the siege of Boonesboro, commissioned "Captain Boone." and later on received a commission as "Major Boone" in the service of the Colonist, or the Revolutionary War, as we now call it." Page 114, *Life of Boone,* by Ellis.

He was notably careless of ever accumulating fortune in lands or lease. After he left Kentucky, his fame attracted Spain to his side, and he went to Missouri. Don Carlos D. Delassus, Lieutenant-Governor for Spain, situated at St. Louis, visited him and presented him with a commission in 1800 as Commandant of the Femme Osage District, an office which included both civil and military duties and honors. Boone discharged the duties of the office, as Commandant and Judge Advocate, with great credit, up to the time when the Territory of Missouri was purchased from Spain by the United States, in 1803, when his office expired. He then retired to his comfortable stone house, built upon a handsome farm in the Femme Osage region, and lived a quiet life of independent ease, enjoying the society of the most learned and distinguished men of that time, who sought to know this nimrod of their century. It was thought he had fought his last battle, but in the War of 1812-15 the old fire of patriotism in his veins impelled him to accept command of the Femine Osage fort. With quenchless courage of other days, he defeated the Indians again, and drove them beyond the Mississippi river. This last feat closed his public career His" wife, Rebecca Bryan Boone, had died in the fall of 1812, and he no longer lived in his own home. She was born in North Carolina, and in June, 1755, married Daniel Boone. She had been a devoted wife and helpmate to the great hunter. Had reared a large family of children, and not only her own, but the children of her widowed brother, James Bryan. She had borne with brave heart the dangers and strange vicissitudes of her husband's life, for which his tardy honors seemed a poor compensation. In sweet and unbroken faith of a better life in the Better Land, she fell asleep. She was buried with unusual ceremonies of love and honor in the neighborhood of her home in the Femme Osage District. Daniel Boone went to live with his son, Nathan Boone, but later on made his home with his daughter and son-in-law, Flanders Callaway. While here, Chester Harding, the celebrated New England artist of that day, visited him for the purpose of painting a portrait of him. Although he was now very feeble, being more than eighty years of age, Daniel Boone consented to a sitting, much to the delight of the artist. A copy of this portrait hangs in the rooms of the Kentucky Historical Society, and is of the same that adorns the first page of this magazine.

In his declining years we are told by a great grand-nephew (who had heard the story from his grandfather, Elijah Bryan), Daniel Boone spent his idle hours carving, with his knife, little souvenirs for his family and friends. On all he would cut his initials or his full name. He gave to his rifles names, it is said, and one of these is in the Historical Society of Missouri, another in the family of a son-in-law in that State, and still another carved by his own hand, is in the Kentucky State Historical Society.

In September, 1820, the famous pioneer was taken ill, and died on the 26th, aged eighty-six years. When his death was announced, the Legislature of Missouri was in session, and adjourned in his honor. His funeral was the largest that had ever been known in the West. He was lamented by his family, as a beloved and honored citizen, a kind father and friend, and by the State as the most famous pioneer in the world. He was buried beside his wife in the wildwood graveyard of the valley of their home in Missouri. There they slept in perfect peace until 1845, when on the 13th of September, their remains were re-interred in the cemetery at Frankfort, Ky., with the grandest procession and most honoring ceremonies that ever attested the admiration of the world for a renowned hero and his wife. We have in our Historical Society a program of that occasion. It reads thus;

Boone
Procession Order.

"It is requested that all business be suspended, and that all persons unite and strictly observe the following order of procession for the re-interment of the remains of the great pioneers of the West, Daniel Boone and his wife, in the Frankfort cemetery grounds, on Saturday, the 13th instant." (13th of September, 1845.)

In 1860, the Legislature of Kentucky directed a monument to be erected over Daniel and Rebecca Boone and in 1862 this monument was completed and erected over their graves by the State of Kentucky. In 1868, the attention of the Legislature was called to this monument. In Collins' History of Kentucky, page 187, vol. 1, we read the Legislature ordered "the monument over Daniel Boone (which had been deferred by Federal soldiers during the war) to be repaired." If this order was ever obeyed, there is no record of it, and certainly no evidence of the repair is there. The chapter of the D. A. R., of Newport, Ky., has undertaken the praiseworthy work of restoring the monument, through subscriptions of the public schools of Kentucky, and their own patriotic endeavors have supplemented the fund for this purpose.

Since every part of the civilized globe has heard the name of Daniel Boone, and bibliographies have compiled the names of the histories written of him, and marble urns and monuments raised to his memory. We see how our great bard, O'Hara, could say of him —

"An empire is his sepulchre;
His epitaph, his fame."

Boone Monument

Erected to his memory in the. Frankfort Cemetery.

In 1910 the above monument was restored, and is now one of the most beautiful monuments in the land.